Gerard Manley Hopkins

A Jesuit in Poets' Corner

by

William Van Etten Casey, S.J.

A Campion Book

Loyola University Press
Chicago, Illinois

Loyola University Press
3441 North Ashland Avenue
Chicago, Illinois 60657

Grateful acknowledgement is made to Robert F. McGovern
for permission to use the reproduction of his original wood-
cut print of Gerard Manley Hopkins.

Library of Congress Cataloging-in-Publication Data

Casey, William Van Etten, 1914–
    Gerard Manley Hopkins: A Jesuit in Poets' Corner
by William Van Etten Casey.
        p.   cm.
    ISBN 0-8294-0636-0
    1. Hopkins, Gerard Manley, 1844-1889, in fiction,
drama, poetry, etc.   I. Title.
PS3553.A79365G47   1990
821'.8–dc20
                                              89-29932
                                              CIP

Contents

Act One

*Musings in the Corner . . . Walt Whitman
and Emily Dickinson . . . the Memorial Tab-
let . . . Ruskin and created beauty . . . the
therapy of wild nature . . . withdrawal and
return . . .* The Wreck of the Deutschland
*. . . the ceremony in Westminster Abbey . . .
Oxford—towery and branchy . . . the path to
Rome . . . parental shock . . . the burden of the
body . . . mortality and immortality.*

Act Two

Friendship with Bridges . . . the "Communist"
letter . . . W. H. Auden and Dylan Thomas . . .
sex and its problems . . . seduced by beauty . . .
North Wales—wild nature . . . South Wales—
polluted nature . . . God—father and headmas-
ter . . . complaint against God . . . to Dublin and
the Irish problem . . . an Englishman in exile . . .
deterioration, desolation, death . . . victory and
the Resurrection.

Preface

Gerard Manley Hopkins died on June 8, 1889. For the centennial commemoration of that event I wrote two pieces that I hoped would serve to introduce this extraordinary English Jesuit poet to a wider audience.

The first was an article which originally appeared in the *Boston College Magazine* (Fall 1988) and is here reprinted, with a few changes and a new title, as Part I of this book. The article is designed both to satisfy and stimulate the reader's curiosity about the poet and his work.

The second was a play written for a single actor who would portray the role of Hopkins discoursing on his life and poetry. The text of the play is now published for the first time and, as Part II, takes up the major portion of this volume. I imagined Hopkins revisiting Poets' Corner in his centennial year and letting his thoughts and words wander in and out of the categories of time—whether past, present, or future—as the mood moved him.

This meant, of course, that I had to invent some ideas and emotions for the ghostly Hopkins. I am sure he will forgive me. I trust the reader will, too. I encourage the reader to become a literary detective and disentangle fact from fantasy in the play.

It was inevitable that an overlap of ideas and words would occur between these two pieces. They were both written by the same person, about the same time, and with the same general audience in mind. I do not apologize for this development; in fact, I defend it by invoking a cherished axiom of the old Jesuit Ratio Studiorum: *repetitio est mater studiorum.*

The text of the play published here is the original text which in some places differs somewhat from the acting script that was used in the performances presented during the centennial year with the title, *Immortal Diamond: A Jesuit in Poets' Corner.* The original text had to be adapted and reduced to an acting script in order to accommodate the exigencies of the stage. The substantial identity between the two texts remains, however, with the reader now having the advantage of a more ample and literary text, whereas the playgoer had the benefit of a more focused and dramatic text.

The play had twenty-five performances in almost as many different cities, where it was very warmly received each time. I am deeply grateful to all my friends who assisted at the creation: in particular, to Michael Moriarty, whose unfailing help supplied "the strong spur, live and lancing like the blowpipe flame . . ."; to Joan Kroc and Lyman Wood, for their generous and timely support; to Joseph Fahey, S.J., and Francis Sweeney, S.J., for Boston College's sponsorship of the première; and to William Cain, S.J., the director, and Henry Wright, the actor, who gave flesh to the word and made it live among us during the centennial year of 1989.

Part I

The Two Lives of
Gerard Manley Hopkins

At high noon on December 8, 1975, in a literary and ecumenical event of major significance, more than 600 persons gathered in Westminster Abbey to honor the Victorian poet Father Gerard Manley Hopkins, S.J. The occasion was the dedication of Hopkins' memorial plaque in Poets' Corner of the Abbey, an event made doubly significant in that it was the centenary both of the wreck of the German ship, the *Deutschland*, in the Thames estuary, and of Hopkins' majestic ode interpreting that tragedy in the context of the Christian faith.

The assembly that day was notable for its distinction as well as its size. Gathered together were the wife of the prime minister, the apostolic delegate, the poet laureate, the Duke of Norfolk, thirteen bishops (mostly Anglican), clergy, religious, poets, actors, reporters, a handful of Hopkins' descendants, and a strong delegation of students from his old school, Highgate.

The night before the ceremony, on BBC radio, the distinguished British actor, Paul Scofield, read Hopkins' longest and greatest poem, *The Wreck of the Deutschland*, in its entirety. During the ceremony itself, Sir John Gielgud, the dean of British actors, read selections from Hopkins' poems, and Peter Levi, professor of poetry at Oxford, gave the principal address.

The Hopkins tablet in Poets' Corner rests between the memorials of the two Victorians, Tennyson and Browning, and the two Moderns, Auden and Eliot. Since Hopkins was born a Victorian and later born again a Modern—the only Victorian to influence twentieth-century poetry—his tablet is strategically situated.

The bust of John Dryden (d. 1700)—before Hopkins, the last Catholic writer to be admitted to this British pantheon—adds a fitting touch to the scene, as it gazes benignly upon the memorial tablet of the only Catholic priest and Jesuit ever enshrined among the greats of English literature.

This honor marked the climax of Hopkins' second life—a life that did not begin until long after his death—when the world of letters finally discovered a major English poet who had lived and died unknown, unhonored, and unsung.

Hopkins' first life had begun in 1844 and ended with his death in 1889. The year 1989 is the centenary of that death and therefore a good time to ponder the mysterious ways of Parnassus and Providence.

His second life began thirty years after his death, with Bridges' publication of his poems in 1918, and it continues to this day without any sign of a *terminus ad quem.* That first edition had a printing of 750 copies, which took ten years to sell out. Today 7,000 copies of the fourth edition of his poems are sold annually.

When Hopkins died one hundred years ago at the age of forty-five, only eleven persons knew that he wrote poetry, and none of them realized that he had a bold and unique talent.   Timid editors rejected his first attempts at publication and so he never tried again.   He developed an ambivalent attitude toward that bitch goddess, fame, and her fickle charms.   "The life I lead is subject to many mortifications, but the want of fame is the least of them," he wrote.   "What I regret is the loss of recognition belonging to the work itself: a great work by an Englishman is like a great battle won by England; it is an unfading bay tree."

At Oxford

When Hopkins at age nineteen went up to Balliol College, Oxford, he was consumed by two passions: the quest for truth, especially religious truth, and the quest for beauty. The first had the priority because life was more important than poetry.   He would have agreed with T. S. Eliot's shrewd observation: "No honest poet can ever feel quite sure of the permanent value of what he has written: he may have wasted his time and messed up his life for nothing."

Gerard's devout parents had reared him carefully in their Anglican faith, but at Oxford he began to feel a powerful pull toward the Roman Catholic Church. He was swept into the turbid wake of the Oxford Movement, that long, spirited, often bitter, debate about the relative religious merits of the Roman Catholic and Anglican traditions.   Hopkins wondered at times whose side, if any, God was on.   Where was *His* music in this din of ecclesiastical bickering?

And Thou art silent, whilst Thy world
Contends about its many creeds. . . .
And truth is heard, with tears impearled,
A moaning voice among the reeds.

Slowly, painfully, he formed his conscience. It became increasingly clear, mathematically clear, he said, that the Roman Catholic Church was the Church founded by Christ and that he had no choice but to embrace it. On October 21, 1866, Father John Henry Newman received him into that church, and he achieved the spiritual peace he had so long sought.

He now faced the unpleasant duty of informing his parents, which he chose to do by letter. The news stunned them. His mother was silent with grief. Not so his father, whose pen flowed with hurt:

Have you not dealt unfairly with your mother and me in leaving us in absolute ignorance? Can you really put aside all our claims upon you by saying that it rests with us to think as you do? All we ask of you is to take so momentous a step with caution and hesitation. Might not our love and our sorrow entitle us to ask this? And you answer by saying that we too could be Roman Catholics, if we pleased, and hence the estrangement is not of your doing. O Gerard, my darling boy, are you indeed gone from us?

This rebuke shook Gerard's heart with tears, but fortunately the love in the Hopkins family was so strong that this estrangement never grew into a serious rupture.

In the nurturing air of Oxford his talents began to flourish. He had the ear of a musician, the hand of a painter, the eye of a naturalist, the tongue of a poet. He could have made his mark in any of these fields, but he chose poetry because it best served his religious interest and his quest for beauty.

The beauty of the world seduced him utterly. He saw, heard, touched, smelled, and tasted this beauty with such clarity and intensity that the world seemed newly minted, freshly made, a paradise of wonder and magic. Every morning, for him, was the first day of creation.

The Drag of the Body

About the time that Gerard's senses were opening wide to the music of the world, he began to experience the dissonance of body and mind that were to plague him for the rest of his life.

> My window shows the travelling clouds,
> Leaves spent, new seasons, alter'd sky,
> The making and the melting crowds:
> The whole world passes; I stand by . . . .
>
> Yet it is now too late to heal
> The incapable and cumbrous shame
> Which makes me when with men I deal
> More powerless than the blind or lame . . . .

Today we would diagnose Hopkins as a neurotic and send him off to a psychiatrist to be cured of his melancholia,

and probably his creativity as well. But he had his own
therapist—nature.

> Then sweetest seems the houseless shore,
> Then free and kind the wilderness.

Wild nature was always able to heal his bruised spirits.
The sight of an unspoiled mountain stream in Scotland
would touch off in him a burst of environmental ecstasy.

> What would the world be, once bereft
> Of wet and of wildness? Let them be left,
> O let them be left, wildness and wet;
> Long live the weeds and the wilderness yet.

He once described the dysfunction of his body and its
nervous system with a stark image drawn from the earth
itself: "In me, nature in all her parcels and faculties gaped
and fell apart, like a clod of earth sticking together and
holding fast only by strings of roots."

His poor body wore him down to such an extent that
he came to despise its flesh and to speak of it in ever more
bitter tones. He referred to it as a burden, a curse, a bad
joke, a fragment of broken pottery, an ill-matched patch of
cloth, a useless splinter of wood, a coffin of weakness and
dejection.

Two months before his death he wrote these lines
that are worthy of the realism of the Book of Ecclesiastes:

> But man—we, scaffold of score brittle bones;
> Who breathe, from groundlong babyhood to hoary
> Age gasp; whose breath is our *memento mori*—
> What bass is *our* viol for tragic tones?
> He! Hand to mouth he lives, and voids with shame . . .

But despite his suffering and these pessimistic views, Hopkins never ceased to find comfort in the doctrine of the resurrection of the body:

> Enough! the Resurrection,
> A heart's-clarion! Away grief's gasping, joyless days,
>   dejection.
>   Across my foundering deck shone
> A beacon, an eternal beam. Flesh fade and mortal trash
> Fall to the residuary worm; world's wildfire, leave but ash:
>   In a flash, at a trumpet crash,
> I am all at once what Christ is, since he was what I am, and
> This Jack, joke, poor potsherd, patch, matchwood, immortal
>   diamond,
>   Is immortal diamond.

After his graduation from Oxford with highest honors, he applied to and was accepted into the English Province of the Society of Jesus. Before entering the Jesuit novitiate that year, he collected the available copies of his poems and burned them. This slaughter of his innocents, as he later referred to it, was not a public histrionic act but a private symbolic gesture reinforcing for himself alone his determination to serve God without reservation. He put his most precious possession, his poetic talent, into God's hands to do with it whatever He wished. He would write no more poetry until he felt he had God's leave for it. That leave did not come until seven years later.

One day in early December of 1875, while Gerard was studying theology at St. Beuno's in North Wales, a ferocious winter storm drove a German ship, the *Deutschland*, off course and onto a treacherous sandbank in the Thames estuary. Howling winds, pounding waves, blinding snow, and bitter cold battered the hapless ship and the terrified passengers for thirty hours.

The British press, especially the *Times*, reported the tragedy in great detail. As all England waited and prayed, the raging sea claimed more than fifty victims, including five Franciscan nuns exiled to America by the German government's new laws against the Catholic Church. The press featured the leader of these nuns, a tall woman, who stood up and dramatically called out to the wild storm: "O Christ, Christ, come quickly!"

The fate of the five nuns and their fellow passengers affected Hopkins deeply, and he said so to his Father Rector, who expressed the hope that someone would write a poem on the subject. That was the hint he had been waiting for. He now felt that he had God's leave to write poems again. He set to work and produced one:

> Thou mastering me
>   God! giver of breath and bread;
>   World's strand, sway of the sea;
>   Lord of living and dead;
> Thou hast bound bones and veins in me, fastened me flesh,
> And after it almost unmade, what with dread,
>   Thy doing: and dost thou touch me afresh?
> Over again I feel thy finger and find thee.

That is the opening stanza of *The Wreck of the Deutschland,* the longest and most ambitious poem (280 lines, six months of composition) that Gerard was ever to write. It is also the most daunting and at the same time the most rewarding religious poem in our literature. In it he realized a new rhythm whose echo had been haunting his ear for the past seven years. He also introduced other new techniques whose boldness demonstrated the truth of John Ruskin's dictum that "a good, stout, self-commanding, magnificent animality is the make for artists and poets."

What kind of reception did it get? The usual one reserved for the daring works of original genius. He sent it to the Jesuit periodical, the *Month,* which at first accepted and then rejected it. One hundred years later the *Month* apologized for that rejection.

Gerard sent his poem to his closest friend, Robert Bridges, who was himself a poet. Bridges hated it, almost as much as he hated the Catholic Church and the Jesuits. He said so bluntly, without regard for Gerard's feelings. "Your full-blooded Roman theology," he wrote, "is bilgewater." And he dismissed the new techniques with one contemptuous word: "jugglery." Bridges added that he would not, for any amount of money, read the poem again.

Hopkins replied by return mail: "Dearest Bridges—I do hope you will read my poem again. Besides money, you know, there is love. Your affectionate friend, Gerard." Killing him softly with his love.

And Bridges did read the poem again—many times—when he was preparing Hopkins' poems for their first publication, a task which he approached quite leisurely. But he still disliked the great ode which he placed in the front of the volume with a warning to the reader to be wary of this "great dragon folded in the gate to forbid all entrance." He used to complain to his friends: "I wish those nuns had stayed at home." And so for some forty years the masterpiece for which Hopkins had such high hopes languished among his papers.

Bridges: The Questionable Friend

Gerard's friendship with Robert Bridges began at Oxford where he was the quiet withdrawn student and Bridges the outspoken gregarious athlete. Although their fundamental differences in temperament, politics, and religion made it an unlikely friendship, it managed to survive the years because of their shared interest in poetry.

At one point it very nearly foundered on a famous "red" letter that Hopkins wrote to Bridges excoriating capitalist England for her callous treatment of the working poor. He became so worked up on the subject that he proclaimed: "Horrible to say, in a way I am a Communist." He was no such thing, of course, but the very conservative Bridges chose to interpret this hyperbolic outburst literally and broke off their friendship for two years. Only Hopkins' initiative in breaking down Bridges' wall of silence by congratulating him on his new book of poems revived their friendship.

Bridges was as conservative in religion as he was in politics. His hostility to Hopkins' religious choices was almost irrational. After Hopkins' death, for example, he wrote to a mutual friend and delivered this outrageous pronouncement on Hopkins' "strange" life: "That dear Gerard was overworked, unhappy, and would never have done anything great seems to give no solace. But how much worse it would have been had his promise or performance been more splendid. He seems to have been entirely lost and destroyed by those Jesuits."

Upon receiving word of Gerard's death, Bridges wrote to the Jesuit superior and asked him to return any of his letters to Gerard which might be left among Gerard's papers. The Jesuit promptly complied and Bridges then destroyed the letters. As a result, we have all of Hopkins' letters to Bridges and (with the exception of three minor ones that somehow escaped) none of Bridges' letters to Hopkins.

Why his unseemly rush? Why his calculated destruction of such valuable material intrinsic to a famous literary friendship? He never explained the reason for his action, but perhaps a clue can be found in the proposal that he made to Gerard's mother about a year later. "I should myself prefer the postponement of the publication of Gerard's poems till I have got my own method of prosody recognised separately from Gerard's. They are the same, and he has the greater claim than I to the origination of it, but he has used it so as to discredit it. A year or eighteen months is all the delay which I expect will be necessary for this." That delay, in fact, lasted almost thirty years. Thus did Salieri scheme to cope with the genius of Mozart.

Even though the only real bond of their friendship was poetry, important differences divided them here. Bridges was an industrious pedestrian poet who thought he possessed a major talent. Hopkins had that talent, but the bold innovations he insisted on sharing with Bridges did not elicit his friend's enthusiasm. Their poetic lives were totally different. Hopkins was a neurotic secret poet, indifferent to the fame that his gifts merited. Bridges was the public published poet, the toast of his time, the poet laureate of England for the last seventeen years of his long life.

But we now look in vain for Bridges' memorial tablet in Poets' Corner among his fellow laureates, Tennyson and Masefield. He would not have believed it possible that his friend Hopkins is there and he is not, that he is now best known, not for his own poems, but as the first editor of Hopkins' poems. "And thus," as Shakespeare noted in *Twelfth Night,* "the whirligig of time brings in his revenges."

Although the two friends were born in the same year, Bridges outlived Hopkins by forty-one years, providentially serving as the bridge between Gerard's two lives. He was a questionable friend and a passable editor, but he did finally publish Hopkins' poems for us.

Life in Wales

Hopkins' Jesuit experience was not a crucifixion, as Bridges frenetically charged, but, as Hopkins himself admitted, a basic fulfillment which he could not otherwise have achieved. The best years of his life, as with so many other Jesuits, were the ten years of his training as a Jesuit—a time of prayer, study, and Jesuit companionship—and for him the best of those years were spent in theological studies at

St. Beuno's College, a Jesuit seminary in North Wales.

> Lovely the woods, waters, meadows, combes, vales,
> All the air things wear that build this world of Wales.

The college, perched on the Clwydian Range, looked out over a wide valley with its two parallel rivers, the wild and romantic Elwy and the more placid Clwyd. He wrote to his father that there was no lovelier spot in all the world. On that "pastoral forehead of Wales" overlooking a "landscape plotted and pieced—fold, fallow, and plough," he began to write poems again, this time with a new, bold, and mature voice.

He studied the Welsh language and its musical poetic forms. He even wrote a few poems in Welsh. Some of his most exuberant nature poetry sprang out of his Welsh experience. North Wales was the true Arcadia of wild nature and became the country of his soul. In later years he would return to St. Beuno's for spiritual and physical refreshment; and as soon as he was back in the Welsh countryside, and saw the hawks flying, and felt again that familiar quiver of ecstasy, he knew that he was home. "I was under a roof here, I was at rest," he wrote.

Gerard had no problems with the Jesuits, but that is not to say that they had no problems with him. Not the usual problems, to be sure. He was a saintly Jesuit: obedient and cooperative, a strict, even a scrupulous observer of the Jesuit vows and rules. If he had been born and bred a Catholic in a Catholic country, he would have been a good candidate for canonization.

The Jesuit problem was to find the right work for him. His personality and presence were somewhat awkward; he was shy and ill at ease in meeting with people. He was not the ideal candidate for the usual categories of Jesuit work. He was a square peg and the Jesuits had only round holes to offer him: teaching, preaching, pastoral care, missionary work. They had no category of work for poets as such. Not that they eschewed poetry or poets: it was simply that for them the writing of poetry would always be an avocation, a sometime thing. The *Times* (London), in its account of the honoring of Hopkins in Poets' Corner, praised him "as the greatest Jesuit poet to emerge from that brilliant but not often poetic Society." The absence of an official Jesuit assignment or designation as a poet did not bother Hopkins in the least. He had no desire to be a working poet—like Bridges. He wanted to be a working priest.

Jesuit superiors moved Hopkins about freely during his years as a working priest in the hope of finding the right slot for his talents. He had seven different assignments in eight years. Gerard never complained to his superiors, but he did rebuke God whom he twice addressed as "sir" with a touch of cool hauteur:

> Thou art indeed just, Lord, if I contend
> With thee; but, sir, so what I plead is just.
> Why do sinners' ways prosper? and why must
> Disappointment all I endeavour end?
>
> Wert thou my enemy, O thou my friend,
> How wouldst thou worse, I wonder, than thou dost
> Defeat, thwart me? Oh, the sots and thralls of lust
> Do in spare hours more thrive than I that spend,
>
> Sir, life upon thy cause . . . .

. . . . birds build—but not I build; no, but strain,
Time's eunuch, and not breed one work that wakes.
Mine, O thou lord of life, send my roots rain.

"It is ironic," Norman MacKenzie writes, "that one of his most enduring poems should be based on the conviction that no work of his would ever endure."

The Dublin Years

God heard his cry, as the Old Testament might have phrased it, and sent him to Ireland where much rain falls upon parched roots. The Jesuit superiors thought they had finally found their answer in the invitation Gerard received to become a fellow of the Royal University of Ireland and professor of Greek at University College, Dublin. At the urging of superiors and after some hesitation on his part he accepted the offer.

For the first two years Gerard handled his new task well enough to make him feel that he might have at last found his proper niche. But during his third year signs of trouble began to show up. The terms of his appointment were—unwittingly—the source of his undoing: not only was he to teach Greek in University College in Dublin but he was also to grade all the Greek exams from the other constituent colleges of Ireland's so-called Royal University. That meant hundreds of exams pouring into his little room all through the year. His desk was always awash with exams to be graded. It was a cruel fate, and for a person of Gerard's acute sense of duty, a crushing burden. As he complained to a friend: "There is nothing like 331 accounts of the Punic Wars—with trimmings—to sweat me down to my lees and low water mudflats with groans and yearnings."

His determination to be scrupulously fair to every exam became an obsession and then a torture. As members of the Examining Board pressed for his grades, he worked in his room with a cold wet towel wrapped around his aching head, trying to meet the deadlines. Anxiety from the relentless pressure of this work gradually wore him down until extreme fatigue and weakness set in. Bouts of undiagnosed fever sent him to the infirmary. Persistent attacks of melancholia deepened into a more dangerous depression. All his go was gone. He was suffering the bitter taste of another defeat.

He recorded these periods of desolation in five late sonnets of such terrible beauty that they still make painful reading today. Their plangent cadences rank with Beethoven's five late quartets and Shakespeare's five late tragedies in their power to express suffering endured and suffering overcome:

Not, I'll not, carrion comfort, Despair, not feast on thee;
Not untwist—slack they may be—these last strands of man
In me ór, most weary, cry *I can no more.* I can;
Can something, hope, wish day come, not choose not to be.

ঙ

O the mind, mind has mountains; cliffs of fall
Frightful, sheer, no-man-fathomed. Hold them cheap
May who ne'er hung there.

ঙ

I wake and feel the fell of dark, not day.
What hours, O what black hours we have spent
This night!
                    . . . .
I am gall, I am heartburn. God's most deep decree
Bitter would have me taste: my taste was me;
Bones built in me, flesh filled, blood brimmed the curse. . .

ঌ

My own heart let me more have pity on; let
Me live to my sad self hereafter kind,
Charitable; not live this tormented mind
With this tormented mind tormenting yet.

In the course of Gerard's fifth year in Ireland, he took
a hard look at his life so far and gave us this frank summary:

At the age of 44 I have been a Catholic for 23 years, a
Jesuit for 21, and a priest for twelve. I never regretted
those decisions, never wavered in my allegiance. But I
was terribly frustrated as a working priest. I have lived
and worked in Ireland for five years, five hard, wearying
wasting wasted years. In those years I did God's will in
the main, and many many examination papers. I did
not blame the Irish for my problems. . . . I needed only
one thing: a working health, a working strength. With
that, any employment would have been tolerable or
pleasant, enough for human nature. However, God did

not see fit to endow me with bodily energy and cheerful spirits. I had to make do without them. But I did not despair and I did keep my sanity. These were my victories.

Not long after this, death came quickly and unexpectedly. He had fallen ill with typhoid fever and was apparently recovering when his condition suddenly worsened. Father Rector notified his parents who rushed from England to his bedside. This upset him at first because he did not wish them to see him so helplessly stricken, but then he realized it was only fitting that they who had bent over him in his first sleep should watch over his last.

On Saturday morning, June 8, 1889, shortly before noon, Father Rector began the traditional Catholic prayers for the dying. Gerard could no longer speak, but he followed the words and responses of his mother and father, deeply grateful that they who had once opposed his acceptance of that faith were now, for these final moments, embracing that faith with him.

Death called at one o'clock. "Thee, God, I come from, to Thee go . . . ." He was now free, free of his coffin of weakness and dejection, free of his body of death.

In a final ironic twist this English superpatriot was buried in the Jesuit plot in Glasnevin, Dublin's public cemetery, surrounded by the monuments of the great Irish patriots—rebels he would have called them—like Wolfe Tone, Charles Parnell, and Daniel O'Connell.

There he rested in obscurity for thirty years until the publication of his poems in 1918 when his second life began. In the most astonishing feat in literary history, he who had been born a Victorian was now born again a Modern, and this time he flourished with such success as a poet that he was eventually enshrined in Poets' Corner.

Gerard would not have been surprised. With his simple clairvoyant faith he had foreseen its possibility: "If the Lord chooses to avail Himself of what I leave at His disposal, He can do so with a felicity and with a success which I could never command."

Part II

A Jesuit in Poets' Corner

PLACE: *WESTMINSTER ABBEY, POETS' CORNER*
TIME: *Now*

Act One

This is the place . . . . . . London's Westminster Abbey—Britain's mother church—where British monarchs from the time of William the Conqueror have been crowned, married, and buried, and where the nation pays tribute to her heroes and great ones. . . . And here, tucked away in a nook of this soaring Gothic cathedral, is Poets' Corner—the pantheon of British letters—where England honors most of her great writers . . . immortals like Chaucer, Shakespeare, Milton, Dickens . . . and a whole breed of lesser immortals.

On the floor, under my feet, a cluster of memorial tablets . . . of Victorians like Tennyson and Browning . . .

of Moderns like Auden and Eliot . . . and here am I—
incredibly—in the midst of them . . . I, Gerard Manley
Hopkins, born a Victorian, but then, two generations
later, born again a Modern.

A peculiar mix . . . here an alcoholic . . . there a homo-
sexual . . . "gay," they call themselves now—a good word
ruined for good . . . over there a social outcast . . . this one
a puritan . . . and that one a roué . . . and I myself, a Jesuit
misfit. . . . Poetics, like politics, makes strange bedfellows.

We're an odd lot . . . scribblers all . . . united in our
passion for the written word. We obeyed the word that the
Lord spoke to the prophet Isaiah:

> And now, go, write it before them on a tablet,
>   and inscribe it in a book,
>   that it may be for the time to come
>   as a witness forever.

Few women grace this national shrine . . . Jane
Austen . . . the Brontë sisters. . . . Over there, on
Robert Browning's tablet—the largest one here—Robert
gets the lion's share of the space, while Elizabeth Barrett,
his wife, is given a brief notice in fine print at the bottom
of his tablet. Why should she be treated as Robert's
appendix? After all, she was the better poet.

Here's a recent arrival . . . Mary Ann Evans, better
known as George Eliot. . . . It took her 100 years after her
death to get here—only 85 for me!—because she had
been socially ostracized by many for having lived with a
married man for twenty-five years and then defending
this union as a permanent and sacred bond. She had a
noble and independent soul, which is revealed in the

quotation that now adorns her memorial tablet. "The first condition of human goodness," she wrote, "is something to love; the second something to reverence." She was a good woman.

Perhaps the most enigmatic occupant of this Corner is a woman named Anne of Cleves. Who was she and what did she write? The answers are: (a) she was the fourth wife of King Henry VIII, and (b) she wrote nothing. Henry had married her, sight unseen, in a match arranged for political purposes by his chief minister, Thomas Cromwell. Anne proved such a dull wife that Henry promptly divorced her and beheaded Cromwell. Anne managed to keep her head, surviving Henry and his five other wives by ten years. She was, apparently, an agreeable sort. She may have written nothing, but here she is. She must have found the formula for survival: "If you can keep your head when all about you are losing theirs," then one day you too might be buried in Poets' Corner.

Another curiosity is the one American poet who is honored here: Henry Wadsworth Longfellow. A popular poet in his time, wealthy and successful. He had some fervent English admirers, but his sentimental moralistic verse has long gone out of fashion. I'm surprised to find him here.

Walt Whitman would have been a better choice of a nineteenth-century American poet than Longfellow. What little I knew of his poetry both attracted and repelled me. I knew in my heart that his mind was more like my own than any other man's living. As he was a great scoundrel, this is not a pleasant confession. This also made me the more desirous to read him—and the more determined that I would not.

Whitman's poetic technique, his marked manner, the original thrust of his mind—all delighted me. His emphasis on the primacy of self struck a responsive chord. He boasted: "I celebrate myself, and sing myself." I like that.

I knew exactly how he felt. When I was young I tried, unsuccessfully, to imagine what it must be like to be someone else.

Like Whitman, I felt the need to proclaim my distinctiveness, to express my uniqueness. I had that sense of self, of *I* and *me*, which is more distinctive than the taste of ale or alum, more unique than the smell of walnut leaf or camphor, and is incommunicable by any means to another person:

> Each mortal thing does one thing and the same:
>   Deals out that being indoors each one dwells;
>   Selves—goes itself; *myself* it speaks and spells,
> Crying *What I do is me: for that I came.*

But Whitman and I parted company over our opposing views of the body and its demands. He stated his creed frankly: "I believe in the body and its appetites: turbulent, fleshly, sensual, eating, drinking and breeding. Copulation is no more rank to me than death is."

While he was in New York singing his song of the flesh, I was in Oxford, trying to sing my song of the spirit by disciplining the flesh and its desires—curbing even my passion for earthly beauty—in an effort to reach a more spiritual level of existence.

Elected Silence, sing to me
And beat upon my whorlèd ear,
Pipe me to pastures still and be
The music that I care to hear.

Shape nothing, lips; be lovely-dumb:
It is the shut, the curfew sent
From there where all surrenders come
Which only makes you eloquent.

Be shellèd, eyes, with double dark
And find the uncreated light:
This ruck and reel which you remark
Coils, keeps, and teases simple sight.

Palate, the hutch of tasty lust,
Desire not to be rinsed with wine:
The can must be so sweet, the crust
So fresh that come in fasts divine!

With the easy confidence of youth I entered into this contest with my body, expecting an early conquest. Although I reflected often on precedents of love, I felt the long success of sin. The lifelong struggle proved exhausting; the final victory elusive.

Even better than Walt Whitman, why not Emily Dickinson as our adopted American poet? I knew nothing of her in my lifetime—who did?—but I learned later that she was a great poet as well as a kindred spirit.

We both lived during the same period of the nineteenth century, born and raised in the warm embrace of upper-middle-class families. And we both became rebels.

During her schooling she said, playfully, that she expected one day to be the belle of Amherst, but she ended up shunning human contact and repudiating her strict religious upbringing. "Some keep the Sabbath going to church," she said. "I keep it staying home."

I went up to Oxford, and although flattered by the renowned Professor Jowett who called me "the star of Balliol," I publicly left the established church of my university, my family, and my country, and entered the disestablished Roman Catholic Church.

Neither of us married. Emily gradually became a recluse in her own home. Although I never became an actual recluse, I was certainly reclusive:

> I have desired to go
>   Where springs not fail,
> To fields where flies no sharp and sided hail
>   And a few lilies blow.
>
> And I have asked to be
>   Where no storms come,
> Where the green swell is in the havens dumb,
>   And out of the swing of the sea.

Emily did not write that. I did.

We were both secret poets. Only eleven people knew that I wrote poetry. Fewer still knew of Emily's gift. Each of us attempted publication early on, but our bold innovations and our verbal intensities drew only negative reactions from timid editors. We quickly withdrew to the higher ground of wounded pride and reflected on fame and her fickle ways.

Emily was contemptuous. "If fame belonged to me," she said, "I could not escape her. If she did not belong to me, my pursuit of her would be futile, and I would forfeit the approbation even of my dog. I prefer my current barefoot state."

My reaction was mixed. The life I led was liable to many mortifications, but the want of fame as a poet was the least of them. What I did regret was the loss of recognition belonging to the work itself. We are Englishmen, and a great poem by an Englishman is like a great battle won by England. It is an unfading bay tree.

Ultimately, fame did come to the two of us—after our deaths—too late to be of any satisfaction to her, too late to be of any spiritual danger to me. It came slowly at first, but then with a felicity and a success that only God could have commanded.

Emily and I shared many of the same themes: suffering and mortality, death and immortality, the seasonal patterns of nature, the burden of the body, faith and God, love and wonder, truth and beauty:

> I died for Beauty—but was scarce
> Adjusted in the Tomb
> When One who died for Truth, was lain
> In an adjoining Room—
>
> He questioned softly "Why I failed"?
> "For Beauty," I replied—
> "And I—for Truth—the two are One—
> We Brethren, are," He said—
>
> And so, as Kinsmen, met a night—
> We talked between the Rooms—
> Until the Moss had reached our lips—
> And covered up—our names—

Emily wrote that. I wish I had.

She is Beauty and he is Truth, and they are together in their tomb. Juliet and her Romeo. A pair of star-cross'd lovers.

But Emily lies in her solitary grave in Amherst with a headstone that carries her own two lovely lonely words— CALLED BACK.

And I? I am lying in my crowded grave in Dublin, an ocean between us. My gravestone is a large cross engraved only with the names and dates of the many Jesuits lying in this common plot, together in our cold celibacy.

In another world—where things could have been so much better arranged than here on this makeshift planet—why could not Emily and I have met—somehow? Why not, O Lord? And would there have been that little flame between us—the flame that ignites the blaze that fuels the fire?

I wonder . . . I wonder . . . O the pity of it!

Ah! My memorial tablet! "A M D G—*Esse Quam Videri*—Gerard Manley Hopkins SJ—1844 – 1889—Priest & Poet—'Immortal Diamond'—Buried at Glasnevin, Dublin"

All the vital facts. Very correct and neat. Excellent taste. Why, even the material of the tablet is right. Basalt—dense, hard, glassy volcanic rock. And black. Black for this cassock that I wear. The American Indians used to call their French Jesuit missionaries "blackrobes." And black for the dark moods of melancholy that plagued me all my life.

A-M-D-G: they stand for the Latin words *Ad Majorem Dei Gloriam*—"For the Greater Glory of God." Ignatius of Loyola, founder of the Jesuits, adopted this Latin motto to epitomize the spirit of his followers. He emphasized that word *majorem*—for the *greater* glory of God. Not any old task that might somehow contribute to the glory of God, but a dynamic imaginative choice of a work that would lead to the *greater* glory of God.

This Ignatian emphasis on the unusual, the unconventional, the imaginative, may explain the large number of Jesuit rebels, mavericks, loners, nonconformists. Even poets. I think it was Diderot who once remarked that you may find every imaginable kind of Jesuit, including an atheist, but you will never find one who is humble.

Esse Quam Videri—another Latin motto. This one from the coat of arms of the Hopkins family. I like that touch—the linking of the mottoes of the two families that meant the most to me—my adopted Jesuit family's A M D G, and my natural family's *Esse Quam Videri*. Ah yes, the translation. "To be rather than to seem." A very good maxim. Wallace Stevens unknowingly translated it when he wrote in one of his poems: "Let be be finale of seem." The real thing, he says, not the appearance of it.

"Gerard Manley Hopkins, SJ"—Do I like my own name? I am neutral on "Gerard." "Manley" I liked, chiefly because it was my father's given name. But "Hopkins" I always disliked. It didn't have the right sound—the syllables too short and light: *"Hop"—"kins."* I wanted something weightier, more resonant and authoritative.

Think of it! How impressive it would have been to have appeared before Queen Victoria with the announcement: "Your Majesty, I have the honor to present to Your Majesty the Jesuit poet, the Reverend Father Gerard Manley FARNSWORTH!" That would have made the royal court sit up and take notice.

"SJ"—two more initials of Latin words: *Societatis Jesu*—"*of* the Society of Jesus." That is to say, a Jesuit. That word—*Jesuit*—was originally used in a negative sense, meaning "a scheming, deceitful fellow," but now we wear it proudly as a badge of honor.

"Priest & Poet"—that's the memorial tablet's summary of my life. These two words are paired neatly enough now, but it was a long hard struggle to bring them comfortably together in my life.

Even as a young student, I had this war within me: between the religious and the poetic, between the sensual and the spiritual, between the ascetic and the aesthetic. There it was, clearly written down in my earliest diaries: "For Lent: no pudding on Sundays, no verses on Fridays." "Today, by God's grace, I resolved to give up all beauty until I had His leave for it."

That was the heart of my conflict: my obsession with beauty, the intensity of my experience of this earth. I was so in love with the loveliness of creation that I feared losing my love of the Creator. I was strained to beauty, but strung by duty.

One of my mentors, John Ruskin, experienced the same conflict. His parents had given him a narrow fundamentalist religious education that created a dilemma for his aesthetic instincts for more than thirty years. But one Sunday in Italy a brilliant illumination flooded his whole being and freed him forever from his prison.

On that morning he had attended a service conducted by an evangelical minister for a tiny congregation in a chapel in the city of Turin. He was disgusted, as he said, "to hear a little squeaking idiot preaching to an audience of seventeen old women and three louts that they were the only children of God in Turin."

Later that afternoon he visited the Gallery in Turin to contemplate the splendor of Paul Veronese's painting of Solomon and the Queen of Sheba. "I was struck," he wrote to his father, "by the gorgeousness of life, which the world seems to be constituted to develop, when it is made the best of . . . . Can it be possible that all this power and beauty is adverse to the honour of the Maker of it? Has God made faces beautiful and limbs strong, and created these strange, fiery, fantastic energies . . . created gold, and pearls, and crystal, and the sun that makes them gorgeous; and filled human fancy with all splendid thoughts . . . only that all these things may lead His creatures away from Him? And is this mighty Paul Veronese, in whose soul there is a strength as of the snowy mountains, and within whose brain all the pomp and majesty of humanity floats in a marshalled glory, capricious and serene like clouds at sunset—this man whose finger is as fire, and whose eye is like the morning—is he a servant of the devil; and is the poor little wretch in a tidy black tie, to whom I listened this Sunday morning expounding Nothing with a twang—is he a servant of God?"

Ruskin's conversion to the acceptance of created beauty as leading *to* rather than away from the Creator came about rather suddenly. Occasionally he would refer to it as his "unconversion." My own unconversion to a similar belief came as a slow dawning that had to be worked out patiently and theologically.

I had other more pressing conflicts that required my immediate attention. One of these was the struggle between the demands of my life and the limitations of my nature. When my studies at Oxford became too burdensome or when excessive human contact wore me down emotionally, I would feel like an alchemist in the city: a man working at the wrong trade in the wrong place. Then I would turn to the healing power of Nature herself.

I could lift these moods only by escaping alone into nature: untouched, untamed, wild nature. That would always free my earthbound spirit and let it soar like the ascending lark to pour and pelt its music till none was left to spill or spend.

> My window shows the travelling clouds,
> Leaves spent, new seasons, alter'd sky,
> The making and the melting crowds:
> The whole world passes; I stand by. . . .
>
> Yet it is now too late to heal
> The incapable and cumbrous shame
> Which makes me when with men I deal
> More powerless than the blind or lame.
>
> No, I should love the city less
> Even than this my thankless lore;
> But I desire the wilderness
> Or weeded landslips of the shore. . . .
>
> And then I hate the most that lore
> That holds no promise of success;
> Then sweetest seems the houseless shore,
> Then free and kind the wilderness.

The beauty of wild nature was a source of deep strength for me. The sight and sound of a mountain stream or brook—what the Scots call a "burn"—on its appointed journey to the lake below, told me eloquently how empty this world would be without its wetlands and its wildlands.

> This darksome burn, horseback brown,
> His rollrock highroad roaring down,
> In coop and in comb the fleece of his foam
> Flutes and low to the lake falls home. . . .
>
> Degged with dew, dappled with dew
> Are the groins of the braes that the brook treads
>   through,
> Wiry heathpacks, flitches of fern,
> And the beadbonny ash that sits over the burn.
>
> What would the world be, once bereft
> Of wet and of wildness? Let them be left,
> O let them be left, wildness and wet;
> Long live the weeds and the wilderness yet.

❧

At the time that I decided to become a Jesuit priest, I was in the early stages of my religious development and naively believed that my priestly vocation was a special grace from God and my poetic nature a threat to that grace. My feelings about this were so strong that an episode in the life of St. Francis of Assisi appealed to me greatly. As the son of a wealthy father, Francis lived a worldly life until his religious conversion in his early twenties. Then he decided upon a dramatic gesture. He strode into the town square, stripped off his rich garments, put on some old rags, and walked away into his new life, a free man.

This inspired me to make my own gesture. Shortly before entering the novitiate I collected all the copies of my poems that I could lay my hands on . . . and burnt them.

> Receive, O Lord, all my liberty, my memory,
> my understanding, and my entire will, all that I have
> and possess. Thou hast given all to me.
> To Thee, O Lord, I return it. Give me Thy love and
> Thy grace, for that is sufficient for me.

This slaughter of my innocents was my young and melodramatic way of renouncing the old and embracing the new.

❧

For seven years I did not write any poems. Then, one day in early December of 1875, while I was studying theology at St. Beuno's Seminary in Wales, a wild winter storm, a Northeast blizzard, drove a German ship, the *Deutschland*, off course and onto the treacherous sandbank known as the Kentish Knock in the mouth of the Thames River. With its propellor broken and its sails useless, the ship was at the mercy of the savage storm. Howling winds, pounding waves, blinding snow, and bitter cold battered the hapless ship and the terrified passengers for thirty hours.

The newspapers reported the ordeal in detail. As all England waited and prayed, the raging sea claimed more than fifty victims, including five Franciscan nuns exiled to America by the German government's new laws against the Catholic Church. The leader of the nuns, a tall woman, was featured in the press because of her loud call for divine aid during the storm. The survivors clung to the stranded wreck until human help finally rescued them.

The reports affected me deeply and I said so to my superior. He expressed the hope that someone would write a poem on the subject. On this hint, I set to work and, though my hand was out at first, produced one. The echo of a new rhythm had long haunted my ear and I now realized it on paper:

> THOU mastering me
> God! giver of breath and bread;
> World's strand, sway of the sea;
> Lord of living and dead;
> Thou hast bound bones and veins in me, fastened me flesh,
> And after it almost unmade, what with dread,
> Thy doing: and dost thou touch me afresh?
> Over again I feel thy finger and find thee.

That is the opening stanza of *The Wreck of the Deutschland,* the longest and most ambitious poem I was ever to write. In it I not only realized that new rhythm but also introduced other innovations whose combined boldness confirmed the truth of John Ruskin's dictum that "a good, stout, self-commanding, magnificent

animality is the make for artists and poets." The
reflections in the poem came from my meditations and
theological studies over those seven silent years. All the
narrative details came from newspaper accounts:

> Into the snows she sweeps,
> Hurling the haven behind,
> The Deutschland, on Sunday; and so the sky keeps,
> For the infinite air is unkind,
> And the sea flint-flake, black-backed in the regular blow,
> Sitting Eastnortheast, in cursed quarter, the wind;
> Wiry and white-fiery and whirlwind-swivellèd snow
> Spins to the widow-making unchilding unfathering deeps.

> She drove in the dark to leeward,
> She struck—not a reef or a rock
> But the combs of a smother of sand: night drew her
> Dead to the Kentish Knock;
> And she beat the bank down with her bows and the ride
> of her keel:
> The breakers rolled on her beam with ruinous shock;
> And canvas and compass, the whorl and the wheel
> Idle for ever to waft her or wind her with, these she endured.

> Hope had grown grey hairs,
> Hope had mourning on,
> Trenched with tears, carved with cares,
> Hope was twelve hours gone;
> And frightful a nightfall folded rueful a day
> Nor rescue, only rocket and lightship, shone,
> And lives at last were washing away:
> To the shrouds they took, —they shook in the hurling and
> horrible airs.

. . . .

They fought with God's cold—
And they could not and fell to the deck
(Crushed them) or water (and drowned them) or
    rolled
With the sea-romp over the wreck.
Night roared, with the heart-break hearing a heart-broke
    rabble,
The woman's wailing, the crying of child without check—
Till a lioness arose breasting the babble,
A prophetess towered in the tumult, a virginal tongue told.

. . . .

Away in the loveable west,
On a pastoral forehead of Wales,
I was under a roof here, I was at rest,
And they the prey of the gales;
She to the black-about air, to the breaker, the thickly
Falling flakes, to the throng that catches and quails
Was calling 'O Christ, Christ, come quickly':
The cross to her she calls Christ to her, christens her wild-worst
    Best.

. . . .

Dame, at our door
Drowned, and among our shoals,
Remember us in the roads, the heaven-haven of the
    reward:
Our King back, Oh, upon English souls!
Let him easter in us, be a dayspring to the dimness of us,
    be a crimson-cresseted east,
More brightening her, rare-dear Britain, as his reign rolls,
    Pride, rose, prince, hero of us, high-priest,
Our hearts' charity's hearth's fire, our thoughts' chivalry's
    throng's Lord.

Well, there's some of it—56 lines from my magnum opus of 280 lines.

&

And what kind of reception did it get? I think you've already guessed. That memory still hurts—more than a hundred years later.

During the six months of its creation I would read the completed parts to a fellow Jesuit who had some poetic talent. He was baffled, and cautioned me against defying all poetic tradition. He advised me to drop all the reflections and make it a straight narrative poem.

A few years after my death, he recalled that experience. "The more Gerard labored at his subject, the more obscure it became," he wrote. "Yet he did not repent. He used to say that for proper appreciation his verses needed to be read aloud by one who has mastered their eccentricities. Well, I heard the poet himself read the *Deutschland* which he was writing at the time, and I could understand hardly one line of it."

I sent the poem to my closest friend, Robert Bridges, who was himself a poet of enough talent to become years later the poet laureate of England. He hated the poem as much as he hated the Catholic Church and the Jesuits, and he said so bluntly without any regard for my feelings. He loathed its full-blooded Roman Catholic theology, which he called "bilgewater." He dismissed all my new poetic techniques with one contemptuous word—"jugglery." He said he would not, for any amount of money, read my poem again.

I replied by return mail: "Dearest Bridges: I do hope you will read my poem again. Besides money, you know, there is love. Your affectionate friend, Gerard."

And he did read my poem again—many times—during the ensuing years, and thirty years after my death he prepared it for its first publication.

I sought publication in a Jesuit periodical called the *Month*. Occasionally it accepted religious verse, mostly treacle and pap:

> Oh, that our souls were gardens
> Of flowers most sweet and rare,
> All watered with tears of penance,
> And nourished with faithful prayer.

So I did not have much hope for the "stout, self-commanding, magnificent animality" of my new voice:

> THOU mastering me
> God! giver of breath and bread;
> World's strand, sway of the sea;
> Lord of living and dead . . .

But the editor, Father Coleridge, surprised and delighted me by promptly accepting my poem for publication in the next issue of the *Month*. You can imagine my disappointment when it did not appear in that issue. Nor in the next. Month after month went by until it became clear that the *Month* had no intention of publishing my poem.

Finally, in a chance encounter with Father Coleridge, I asked him frankly what had wrecked my *Wreck*.

"I found your poem fascinating, Gerard, at least those parts I could understand. But my two assistant editors voted firmly against publication. They said our readers were not yet ready for your subtle thinking and your daring experiments. What is the purpose, for example, of all those accents sprinkled through every line of your poem? I found them rather distracting."

"They indicate the stresses to be observed in following my new rhythm, which I call sprung rhythm. It is closer to the natural rhythm of speech than the traditional running rhythm of English poetry. My poems are like music—they are intended to be heard with the ear, not just read with the eye. They must be spoken to have their meaning clear and their emotion felt."

"And all those strange words. Where did you find them?"

"Some words I coined; others I designed from existing words; and some are dialect words. Above all, I love the one-syllable Anglo-Saxon words of our language. They give power and beauty to a poem. Words are like diamonds. Compression increases their potency and brilliance. That sparkle and that punch excite me very much. Listen: fling, ring, sing; dim, trim, grim; take, make, sake; drink, wink, sink; gay, gang, gash; blush, gush, flush; soar, roar, score; steep, creep, weep; luck, tuck, ruck; doom, loom, bloom; latch, catch, snatch; tall, fall, gall. Shall I go on?"

"Not necessarily," Father Coleridge said, as we parted with an amicable handshake and an exchange of smiles.

My entire experience of the wreck of the *Deutschland* proved to be a turning point. Now that I had my superior's favorable word, I felt free to write poems as my muse might move me and my priestly duties allow.

I was determined to continue on in my new voice and to develop new poetic theories and techniques. "What I do is me: for that I came."

The episode with the *Month* convinced me that God was warning me against the pursuit of personal fame and worldly recognition. I decided instead to entrust my poems to Robert Bridges for criticism, safekeeping, and possible future publication.

Those assistant editors of the *Month* were right, the audience for my bold innovations was not there at that time. Perhaps a distant generation might find some merit in my poems. That generation proved to be very distant indeed.

Bridges did publish my poems, thirty years after my death, in an edition of 750 copies. It took ten years to sell out that first edition. Slowly, unobtrusively, over the next forty years, I crept into full recognition as a poet.

The climax came eighty-five years after my death with the ceremony in Westminster Abbey welcoming me here to Poets' Corner. The fame that I had shunned during life arrived that day in a sudden heady rush.

The date was Monday, December 8, 1975, exactly one hundred years to the day that the German ship foundered at our very door.

At high noon more than 600 people of all faiths and no faith—bishops, clergy, professors, politicians, journalists, actors, writers, poets, celebrities, a handful of my descendants, and even a strong delegation of boys from my old Highgate School—all gathered to usher me into Poets' Corner with due pomp and circumstance.

The harmonic originality of Henry Purcell's "Trumpet Tune and Air"—my beloved Purcell, whose monument is over there in the north aisle—lifted our spirits with the clarity and purity of his air of angels.

The congregation sang the hymn, "Praise to the Holiest in the Height," composed by John Henry Cardinal Newman, who in the year of my birth had shocked the Church of England by his public conversion to the Church of Rome.

The Dean of Westminster welcomed us all with gracious words and ecumenical sentiments.

Sir John Gielgud, the actor, read from my poems in his tenor voice, "that silver trumpet muffled in silk."

The Duke of Norfolk, England's ranking Catholic layman, unveiled my memorial, saying: "In gratitude for the poetry of Gerard Manley Hopkins I ask the Dean and Chapter of Westminster to receive this memorial into their safe custody."

The Dean replied: "To the greater glory of God and in honor of Gerard Manley Hopkins we accept this memorial and dedicate it, in the name of the Father, and of the Son, and of the Holy Spirit. Amen."

My oldest surviving relative, a grandnephew named after my youngest brother, Lionel, placed a wreath on the memorial.

Peter Levi, the poet, preached a lyrical address on a text from the Book of Revelation: "Him that overcometh will I make a pillar in the temple of my God, and he shall go no more out: and I will write upon him the name of my God."

I watched the whole ceremony from behind the monument of John Dryden, the last Roman Catholic to be honored here—almost 300 years ago. Fortunately,

I was out of my body. If I had been confined to that coffin of weakness and dejection, I probably would have lost control, maybe even have fainted. Instead, I looked and listened impassively, with a calm spiritual detachment.

> I am soft sift
> In an hourglass—at the wall
> Fast, but mined with a motion, a drift,
> And it crowds and it combs to the fall;
> I steady as a water in a well, to a poise, to a pane,
> But roped with, always, all the way down from the tall
> Fells or flanks of the voel, a vein
> Of the gospel proffer, a pressure, a principle, Christ's gift.

And so the day ended, leaving me the only Catholic priest and Jesuit ever honored in this Anglican shrine.

And so too came fame, finally, but with that felicity and success which, as I said, only God could have commanded.

❧

The American Jesuits, with their fondness for baseball metaphors, describe the lengthy probationary period in the making of a Jesuit as a long wind-up followed by a wild pitch.

Am I that wild pitch? For the Anglicans, yes, because I went over to the Catholics and the Jesuits. For the Catholics and the Jesuits, also yes, because I have now ended up enshrined in this Anglican mother church of Britain.

When I told my adviser, Father Newman, of my decision to be a Jesuit, despite my misgivings about my ability to take the difficult Jesuit discipline, he said: "Don't call the Jesuit discipline hard. It will bring you to heaven."

Bring me to *heaven*? Is this Abbey and its glorious history what he had in mind?

Later, when I became first a Catholic and then a Jesuit, I knew that these decisions would be a terrible blow to my parents. They were devout Anglicans who brought up their eight children very carefully in the Anglican faith. Since I was the eldest child, they expected me to lead the others by my example, and they secretly hoped that I would eventually choose the Anglican priesthood. But I began to develop an interest in the Roman Catholic Church because I felt that I could do the will of God more faithfully in that Church. The Catholic Church was the mother of saints, and I wanted to be . . . a saint . . . not a poet. At Oxford these sentiments bloomed and flourished. Oxford! It was not just a university town; it was a shining city set upon a hill.

When I first caught sight of Oxford:

> Towery city and branchy between towers;
> Cuckoo-echoing, bell-swarmèd, lark-charmèd, rook-
>   racked, river-rounded . . .

and breathed its

> Wild air, world-mothering air,
> Nestling me everywhere . . .

I was very excited, and felt that momentous changes were in store for me.

I was soon swept into the turbid wake of the Oxford Movement, that long, spirited, often bitter controversy about the relative religious merits of the Roman Catholic and Anglican traditions. Of the original leaders of the movement, only Pusey was still active within the university when I arrived. Newman continued to be a saintly and articulate voice—outside the university. Battle lines had been drawn. Arguments marshalled. Feelings high. Friendships shattered. Lives changed. "Heartbreaking things I saw with my own eyes and was myself a part of." I wondered often whose side, if any, God was on.

> And Thou art silent, whilst Thy world
> Contends about its many creeds
> And hosts confront with flags unfurled
> And zeal is flushed and pity bleeds
> And truth is heard, with tears impearled,
> A moaning voice among the reeds.

My conscience became more and more deeply involved. Where was the music of God in this din of ecclesiastical bickering? I began to hear the authentic cadence ever more clearly.

> I have found my music in a common word,
> Trying each pleasurable throat that sings
> And every praisèd sequence of sweet strings,
> And know infallibly which I preferred . . .
> I have found the dominant of my range and state—
> Love, O my God, to call Thee Love and Love.

Every week my desire to embrace the Roman Catholic faith openly became stronger. The final decision came in a rush. My heart, being hard at bay was out with it!

> How a lush-kept plush-capped sloe
> Will, mouthed to flesh-burst,
> Gush!—flush the man, the being with it,
> Brim, in a flash, full!

Then came the dread duty of telling my parents of my decision. This I chose to do by letter. I simply could not have coped with the emotions stirred up by a face-to-face meeting. The news, as expected, stunned them. Mother was silent with grief. Father's pen flowed with hurt:

One thing more, Gerard. Have you not dealt unfairly with your mother and me in leaving us in absolute ignorance until your decision was finally taken? . . . Are we not justified in asking you to pause? Can you really put aside all our claims upon you by saying that it rests with us to think as you do? The manner in which you seem to repel and throw us off cuts us to the heart. All we ask of you is for your own sake to take so momentous a step with caution and hesitation. Have we not the right to do this? Might not our love and our sorrow entitle us to ask it? And you answer by saying that we too could be Romanists, if we pleased, and hence the estrangement is not of your doing. O Gerard, my darling boy, are you indeed gone from us?

His letter shook my heart with tears. I could only remind myself of Christ's claim upon his disciples: "I came not to send peace, but a sword. For I am come to set a man at variance against his father. And a man's foes shall be they of his own household. He that loveth father or mother more than me is not worthy of me. He that loseth his life for my sake shall find it."

How to explain such an emotional reaction from my parents?

The average English mind of that time, conditioned by bitter memories of the national struggle between Catholics and Reformers, contemned Catholicism as the church of that lowly and fractious minority, the Irish.

The more apocalyptic among those minds fed on the Book of Revelation and equated the Catholic Church with the Scarlet Woman of Babylon and the Pope with the Great Whore of Rome.

My parents were not *that* benighted, of course, but neither could they totally escape the inherited views of their anti-Catholic nationalism.

That's why my father wrote to me as though I had planned to elope with a prostitute.

Fortunately, the temporary estrangement did not grow into a serious rupture. Our love was too strong for that. And they were relieved to learn that I would finish my studies at Oxford. They accepted me back into the family, even if they could not accept my decision.

And that decision never wavered, either then or thereafter. Father John Henry Newman received me into the Catholic Church on October 21, 1866, and I achieved the spiritual peace I had so long sought.

My next decision, to become a Jesuit priest, met little vocal resistance from my parents who had now resigned themselves to my headstrong ways. This was surprising because the Jesuits had an unsavoury reputation, even among the educated English.

Robert Bridges wrote to a mutual friend after my death: "Dear Gerard was overworked, unhappy and would never have done anything great. He seems to have been entirely lost and destroyed by those Jesuits."

On the same occasion another old university friend wrote to my brother: "Gerard made a grievous mistake in joining the Jesuits whose system has killed many and many a noble soul. To get on with the Jesuits you must become a machine—without will, without conscience—and that, to his nature, was an impossibility. To his lasting honour be it said he was too good for them."

But opposition to the Jesuits did arise within my family—this time from an unexpected quarter. My younger brother, Lionel, fifteen years old, took me aside one day and said earnestly: "Gerard, Catholics may be all right—but Jesuits? No! They're a disreputable lot. You can't be serious."

I put my arm around his shoulder and replied with equal earnestness: "Lionel, if you should think of visiting Parliament when it opens next year, don't do it. I am joining an international gang of terrorists who plan to blow up the whole damn place that day. Another Gunpowder Plot masterminded by the Jesuits!"

Instead of visiting Parliament that year Lionel came to see me in the Jesuit novitiate.

Lionel early gave up Anglicanism for agnosticism, despite his careful religious upbringing by our parents. He entered the British Consular Service in China, retired and became a scholar of worldwide reputation of the Chinese language. He died in our family home in Haslemere at the ripe old age of ninety-eight. He never married. And he never became a Jesuit.

ŵ

All the members of my large family, except an infant son and myself, lived long lives. The first prize went to mother. She lived to be ninety-nine—a remarkable age for a woman of those times who had borne nine children. My parents gave me every good thing except the gift of their own robust health.

From the beginning I had to endure fragile health and an overwrought nervous system. In me, nature in all her parcels and faculties gaped and fell apart, like a clod sticking together and holding fast only by strings of roots. One ailment after another. Aches and pains. Fatigue and fevers. Scrupulosity and sultry sieges of melancholy. Sharp swings between high and low spirits.

For me, the body was a burden, a curse, a jackass, a bad joke, a piece of broken pottery, an ill-matched piece of cloth, a jagged splinter of perishable wood, a scaffold of poor brittle bones, a coffin of weakness and dejection. I longed to be out of it. I was "half in love with easeful Death."

When I worried that the Jesuit discipline might be too hard for me, I did not doubt my ability, with God's grace, to observe the vows and rules. I feared that "the jading and jar of the cart, time's tasking," the daily relentless grind of work and study and prayer, would wear down my body and mind to the breaking point. My experience at Oxford had warned me of this danger. The odor of death and decay is always with us.

In a touching scene near the end of *King Lear* the blind Gloucester meets his old king, now mad and dying. He recognizes the king's voice and exclaims: "O, let me kiss that hand!" Lear draws back.   "Let me wipe it first," he says, "it smells of mortality."   Only man knows that smell:

> A dog
> that dies
> and that knows
> that it dies
> like a dog
> and that can say
> that it knows
> that it dies
> like a dog
> is a man.

I knew that smell of mortality from my earliest youth.   I long had in my mind the image of a young child—perfect in the freshness of her all-youth, the flower of beauty in her winning ways, her innocent airs, maiden manners, sweet locks, loose locks, long locks, lovelocks, gaygear, going gallant, girlgrace.   She is standing, alone, in a grove during the autumn of the year, a thoughtful look upon her face.   The setting sun bathes the scene in a shimmering golden light as the dying leaves flutter down about her.   In the blooming beauty of her own personal spring, amid the fading beauty of nature's fall, I ask her:

Márgarét, áre you gríeving
Over Goldengrove unleaving?
Leáves, líke the things of man, you
With your fresh thoughts care for, can you?
Áh! ás the heart grows older
It will come to such sights colder
By and by, nor spare a sigh
Though worlds of wanwood leafmeal lie;
And yet you *will* weep and know why.
Now no matter, child, the name:
Sórrow's spríngs áre the same.
Nor mouth had, no nor mind, expressed
What heart heard of, ghost guessed:
It ís the blight man was born for,
It is Margaret you mourn for.

In my various assignments as a parish priest
ministering to the working poor in cities like Liverpool
and Glasgow, I frequently attended to the spiritual needs
of the sick and dying among these unfortunate people.
I remember one in particular: Felix Randal, a farrier,
a blacksmith who shoed horses. At the age of thirty-one,
in the pride of prime's enjoyment, pulmonary
tuberculosis—a common disease of the poor—struck him
down.

I visited him regularly, brought him Holy
Communion, and when the time came, anointed him for
his final journey. A bond of affection developed between
us.

As he lay there in his weakness, his mind wandered back to the days of his strength when he made heavy iron shoes for large powerful draft horses. Or so *he* thought. I saw him at work in the smithy of the gods, fashioning delicate shoes for Pegasus, the wingèd horse of Greek mythology. This magical creature, with a single slash of his bright and battering hoof caused the sacred fountain of the Muses to gush forth on Mount Helicon and become the source of poetic inspiration.

Then one day word came that Felix had died.

Felix Randal the farrier, O is he dead then? my duty all ended,
Who have watched his mould of man, big-boned and hardy-
      handsome
Pining, pining, till time when reason rambled in it and some
Fatal four disorders, fleshed there, all contended?

Sickness broke him. Impatient, he cursed at first, but mended
Being anointed and all; though a heavenlier heart began some
Months earlier, since I had our sweet reprieve and ransom
Tendered to him. Ah well, God rest him all road ever he
      offended!

This seeing the sick endears them to us, us too it endears.
My tongue had taught thee comfort, touch had quenched thy
      tears,
Thy tears that touched my heart, child, Felix, poor Felix
      Randal;

How far from then forethought of, all thy more boisterous
      years,
When thou at the random grim forge, powerful amidst peers,
Didst fettle for the great grey drayhorse his bright and battering
      sandal!

❧

Death is so devastating that we try to cover up its grim reality with bland words. Take Henry James, a master of subtle thought and refined prose, who is memorialized here in Poets' Corner. When a stroke felled him late in life he said to a friend: "So it has come at last—the Distinguished Thing." He lingered on until "the Distinguished Thing" carried him off. In a word, he died. "Dead"—the finality of the word itself matches the finality of the event.

Death is a braggart, pretending that he alone has complete dominion over life, boasting of the violent instruments at his command:

> 'Some find me a sword; some
> The flange and the rail; flame
> Fang, or flood' goes Death on drum,
> And storms bugle his fame.
> But wé dream we are rooted in earth—Dust!
> Flesh falls within sight of us, we, though our flower the same,
> Wave with the meadow, forget that there must
> The sour scythe cringe, and the blear share come.

Death may have universal dominion over life, but is that dominion final, absolute and independent? Is there anyone anywhere who has dominion over Death itself? Is there one such? Yes, there is one, I have One, only not within the seeing of the sun, not within the singeing of the strong sun . . . somewhere elsewhere there is One, One. . . *He* has dominion over Death. . . *He* is Lord of living and dead:

I admire thee, master of the tides,
      Of the Yore-flood, of the year's fall;
  The recurb and the recovery of the gulf's sides,
        The girth of it and the wharf of it and the wall;
  Stanching, quenching ocean of a motionable mind;
  Ground of being, and granite of it: past all
        Grasp God, throned behind
Death with a sovereignty that heeds but hides, bodes but
    abides.

God has the dominion over Death, and He has
made the human soul immortal. But is that all? Is that
enough? What happens to this bone-house, this mean
house where man's mounting spirit dwells? What about
this sack of frail clay, foul clay, that burdens my whole
life?

I found my answer in St. Paul. The trumpet shall
sound, he said, and the dead shall be raised incorruptible,
and we shall be changed. This mortal dust shall put on
immortality, and Death shall be swallowed up in victory.
Thanks be to God, which giveth us the victory through our
Lord Jesus Christ:

            Enough! the Resurrection,
A heart's-clarion! Away grief's gasping, joyless days, dejection.
            Across my foundering deck shone
A beacon, an eternal beam. Flesh fade and mortal trash
Fall to the residuary worm; world's wildfire, leave but ash:
            In a flash, at a trumpet crash,
I am all at once what Christ is, since he was what I am, and
This Jack, joke, poor potsherd, patch, matchwood, immortal
    diamond,
            Is immortal diamond.

Act Two

My friendship with Robert Bridges began at Oxford where he was well known as an athlete, the stroke of the crew, and I was less well known as a student. We were drawn together by our common interests in religion, politics, and poetry, but in each of them we soon found that we had profound differences. But I would not let any disagreement disrupt our friendship. This was not easy with a man like Bridges whose views on any subject were firmly set in cement and just as firmly and loudly expressed.

We were both Anglicans—High Church, but he was well satisfied with things as they were while I was restless and searching. He deplored my Roman leanings. After I became a Catholic and a Jesuit, I discovered how much he hated Catholics and loathed Jesuits. But I still kept up our friendship.

In politics we both began as Tories, but in time he became more conservative as I became more liberal. This development at one point nearly ended our friendship. It came about from a letter I wrote to him when I became aware of the living conditions of the poor in our northern cities. I began to have radical views and feelings about the obvious injustices in our capitalist society. One day, in a depressed and angry mood, I sat down and wrote to him:

> Dearest Bridges:
> My experience has utterly convinced me of the misery of life for the poor, of the degradation of our race, and of the hollowness of this century's civilisation. I find life a burden to have daily thrust upon me the things I see. Horrible to say—in a way, I am a Communist. Their ideal is nobler than that professed by any statesman I know of. Besides it is just, although I do not mean that their methods of getting to it are. But it is a dreadful thing for the working poor of a very rich nation to live so hard a life without dignity, without knowledge, without comfort or delights or hopes—and that in the midst of plenty—a plenty which they help to make. England has grown hugely wealthy, but this wealth has not reached the working classes.
>
> Believe me your affectionate friend.
> Gerard Hopkins, S.J.

Well, that nearly did it. That would have ended our friendship, had I let it. After that letter . . . two years of silence. Nothing. I finally broke *his* long silence by writing to congratulate him when I read a review of a new book of poems that he had recently published. He replied promptly to *that*. And so we resumed our correspondence and friendship, but he never once acknowledged or referred to my so-called "Communist" letter. Bridges did not hesitate to deliver himself of strong opinions bluntly stated, but he refused to grant others a like privilege.

Poetry was the real bond of our friendship. We exchanged poems and criticized each other's work. But poetry for me was strictly an avocation. For Bridges, it became his whole life. When he came into his inheritance early, he gave up the practice of medicine and took up the life of a country gentleman and a professional poet.

During our lives I was the secret unknown poet and he the successful public poet, the toast of his time. But history has its ironies. I look in vain for his memorial tablet here among his fellow laureates, Tennyson and Masefield. He must find it odd, to say the least, that I am here and he is not. I would like to hear his strong blunt opinion on that.

Despite our religious and political disagreements, our friendship endured. I wanted it to endure. I needed him. He became the sounding board for my poetic theories and experiments, my only link to the larger artistic world, my only editor, and my entire public. I wrote for him and he saved my poems. And I wanted him to become a Roman Catholic!

He did publish my poems—finally. He certainly took his time about it: thirty years after my death. And he still harbored doubts about my *Wreck of the Deutschland,* which he put in the front of the first edition, with a warning to the reader to be wary of "this great dragon folded in the gate to forbid all entrance." He used to say to his friends: "I wish those nuns had stayed at home."

It was thoughtful of him to dedicate the first edition to my mother, at that time ninety-eight years old. The dedication was written in Latin by A. E. Housman, the poet and scholar, who had a low opinion of my poetic technique.

Bridges himself composed a touching prefatory sonnet in my memory. Its final two lines sent me to my fate in the world of poetry with these words:

> Go forth: amidst our chaffinch flock display
> Thy plumage of far wonder and heavenward flight!

"Our chaffinch flock," he wrote. The finch is a very common British songbird, and I suppose we have a good collection of them right here in this aviary.

Over there is Lord Byron's memorial inscribed with a few lines of his best bombast:

> But there is that within me
>   which shall tire
> Torture and Time and breathe
>   when I expire.

His tablet is white, pure white Carrara marble. I wonder who chose that color for *him.*

Two rare birds are side by side with me. On this side, W. H. Auden, a man with a double life, hinted at in his own couplet inscribed on his memorial tablet:

> In the prison of his days
> Teach the free man how to praise.

He was a professed and active homosexual. When he went to the United States at the age of thirty-two he fell in love with a young man of eighteen who became the grand passion of his life. He considered himself married to this youth whose early infidelities almost provoked Auden to murder him. But throughout his life he remained a faithful and committed Christian. . . . "In the prison of his days / Teach the free man how to praise."

On the other side is Dylan Thomas. He burst upon the scene in 1950 when he arrived at a New York party on West Eleventh Street and loudly announced: "I am Dylan Thomas. First, I'm a Welshman. Second, I'm a drunkard. Third, I'm a heterosexual."

He became a celebrity as he went about giving readings and getting drunk and cutting an erotic swath all down the East Coast. At age thirty-nine, in New York City, he died suddenly, not from too much adulation, as a friend suggested, but from an insult to the heart, as the coroner reported, caused by eighteen straight whiskies to the mouth.

Despite the scandal of his last years, he arrived here in this shrine only thirty years after his death. It took me eighty-five. Why the difference? Well . . . he had a president of the United States pushing his cause. I had only the Holy Spirit lobbying for me. . . . His memorial tablet carries two of his most poetic lines:

> Time held me green and dying
> Though I sang in my chains like the sea.

Yes, he was as green as his native land, as wild as the stormy sea, and bound by the appetites that led to his premature death. But how he did sing in his chains!

Auden in his prison. Thomas in his chains. . . . And I? . . . Also a prisoner . . . of the body . . . "cabin'd, cribb'd, confin'd." . . . A caged skylark, sometimes singing sweetly, sometimes drooping deadly, sometimes wringing my barriers in bursts of fear or rage.

So here I am! . . . a vowed celibate . . . honored together with a professed homosexual on one side and a proclaimed heterosexual on the other. How odd! Three poets . . . all in a row . . . each with a different orientation to sex . . . to the other sex . . . to the same sex . . . to no sex. . . . It's hard to say which of us had the more problems.

🔹

When I became a Jesuit I took the vow of chastity, which included the obligation of celibacy. Ignatius of Loyola was not a model of chastity in *his* early youth, but in his rules for his followers he was brief, blunt, and uncompromising on that subject. "What concerns the vow of chastity needs no explanation," he wrote, "as it is plain how perfect should be its observance by a serious endeavor to imitate the purity of the angels in cleanness of both body and mind." Period. *That* takes care of *that* problem. Oh well. That also takes care of some other problems: all those nasty diseases that people give to each other—lymphogranuloma venereum, pediculosis pubis, molluscum contagiosum, syphilis, gonorrhea, and so on and so forth. From all the perils of sexual congress, deliver us, O Lord.

My problem was not sex. It was the intensity of my experience of this world. Joy in the earth and all her creatures would naturally flow into delight in man and woman and their beauty, both of mind and body. I think that no one can admire beauty of the body more than I do, but this kind of beauty is dangerous, sets the blood dancing.

At one time I had thought of a career in painting, but rejected that idea because the higher and more attractive parts of the art put a strain upon the passions which I should think would have been unsafe to encounter.

No . . . it was not sex. . . . My real problem was . . . simply . . . beauty. The beauty of this world seduced me utterly. My attraction for beauty . . . for any form of beauty . . . was so compelling that it threatened to undermine my faith, and even my mind. I did not know how to cope with it. I saw, heard, felt, tasted, and smelled this beauty with such clarity and intensity that the world seemed newly minted, freshly made, a daily source of extraordinary magic and wonder.

I found it in the first smile that steals over the infant's face . . . in the childhood bloom of a dappled die-away cheek and wimpled lip . . . in limber liquid boys swimming in the river with dare and downdolphinry, and bell-bright bodies huddling out . . . in girls with their dearly and dangerously sweet fleece of beauty fleeing . . . in Felix Randal, big-boned and hardy-handsome . . . in Harry Ploughman's hard-as-hurdle arms, rack of ribs, scooped flank, lank rope-over thigh, knee-nave and barrelled shank . . . in the new moon, dwindled and thinned to the fringe of a fingernail held to the candle . . . in the all roar of the storm and the beat of endragoned seas . . . in the night, with its belled fire and moth-soft Milky Way . . . in clouds, those dazzling puffballs, torn tufts, tossed pillows, heaven-roysterers, gay gangs scampering down air-built thorough-fares . . . in the skylark's rash-fresh music and the woodlark's tiny trickle of a song-strain . . . in the candycoloured, gluegold-brown, marbled river, boisterously beautiful . . . in the faint honey smell and sweet gum taste of the bluebell . . . in my aspens dear, whose airy cages quelled or quenched in leaves the leaping sun . . . in all that my eyes saw, wandering on the world.

> Glory be to God for dappled things—
>   For skies of couple-colour as a brinded cow;
>   For rose-moles all in stipple upon trout that swim;
> Fresh-firecoal chestnut-falls; finches' wings;
>   Landscape plotted and pieced—fold, fallow, and plough;
>   And áll trádes, their gear and tackle and trim.
>
> All things counter, original, spare, strange;
>   Whatever is fickle, freckled (who knows how?)
>   With swift, slow; sweet, sour; adazzle, dim;
> He fathers-forth whose beauty is past change:
>   Praise him.

To what purpose all this enchanting mortal beauty? It warms our wits to the changeless Immortal Beauty behind it. But what should we *do* with this created beauty? Simply love it, accepting heaven's sweet gift. Use it. Then leave it. Confess its divine origin. Our duty but to offer all this beauty *back* . . . back to God, beauty's self and beauty's giver. Then wish for everyone God's better beauty—His grace.

I certainly wished God's better beauty for Dylan Thomas. He may have been a prodigal son, but he was a son of Wales, and I was in love with all things Welsh.

I spent the three happiest years of my life at St. Beuno's College in North Wales. This Jesuit theological seminary was perched on the Clwydian Range overlooking the vale with its two parallel rivers, the wild and romantic Elwy and the more placid Clwyd. There's no more beautiful spot on all the earth.

Lovely the woods, waters, meadows, combes, vales,
All the air things wear that build this world of Wales.

On that loveable pastoral forehead of Wales I began to write poetry again, starting with *The Wreck of the Deutschland*. I studied the Welsh language and its musical poetic forms. I even wrote a few poems in Welsh. Some of my more exuberant nature poems sprang out of my Welsh experience. The arrival of spring always excited my muse:

Nothing is so beautiful as Spring—
>   When weeds, in wheels, shoot long and lovely and
>   lush;
>   Thrush's eggs look little low heavens, and thrush
Through the echoing timber does so rinse and wring
The ear, it strikes like lightnings to hear him sing;
>   The glassy peartree leaves and blooms, they brush
>   The descending blue; that blue is all in a rush
With richness; the racing lambs too have fair their fling.

What is all this juice and all this joy?
>   A strain of the earth's sweet being in the beginning
In Eden garden. . . .

One clear night in August, as we drove home in our
open cart, the stars came out thick: I leaned back to look
at them and my heart, opening more than usual, praised
the Lord to and in whom all that beauty comes home:

Look at the stars! look, look up at the sky!
>   O look at all the fire-folk sitting in the air!
>   The bright boroughs, the circle-citadels there!
Down in dim woods the diamond delves! the elves'-eyes!

>   ❧

>   I kiss my hand
>   To the stars, lovely-asunder
>   Starlight, wafting him out of it; and
>   Glow, glory in thunder;
Kiss my hand to the dappled-with-damson west:
Since, tho' he is under the world's splendour and wonder,
>   His mystery must be instressed, stressed;
For I greet him the days I meet him, and bless when I
>   understand.

On another late summer's morning I went fishing alone in the river Elwy, and as I walked home, absorbing the beauty of that September day, I suddenly experienced a half-hour of extreme enthusiasm:

> Summer ends now; now, barbarous in beauty, the
>   stooks rise
> Around; up above, what wind-walks! what lovely
>   behaviour
> Of silk-sack clouds! has wilder, wilful-wavier
> Meal-drift moulded ever and melted across skies?
>
> I walk, I lift up, I lift up heart, eyes,
> Down all that glory in the heavens to glean our
>   Saviour;
> And, éyes, heárt, what looks, what lips yet gave you a
> Rapturous love's greeting of realer, of rounder
>   replies?. . . .

In later years I would return to St. Beuno's for physical and spiritual refreshment, and as soon as I was in the Welsh countryside, and saw the hawks flying and felt that little quiver of ecstasy, I knew I was home. I found that ecstasy, real ecstasy—which by nature is short-lived—came to me best when I was alone. I need to be alone with a feeling of leisure—all pressure taken off—to savor the emotion of the moment. I had such a feeling whenever I could watch at close range that wonder of wild and free nature, the windhover or falcon, in the act and art of flying:

I caught this morning morning's minion, king-
   dom of daylight's dauphin, dapple-dawn-drawn Falcon, in
   his riding
   Of the rolling level underneath him steady air, and
   striding
High there, how he rung upon the rein of a wimpling wing
In his ecstasy! then off, off forth on a swing,
   As a skate's heel sweeps smooth on a bow-bend: the hurl
   and gliding
   Rebuffed the big wind. My heart in hiding
Stirred for a bird,—the achieve of, the mastery of the thing!

Brute beauty and valour and act, oh, air, pride, plume, here
   Buckle! AND the fire that breaks from thee then, a billion
Times told lovelier, more dangerous, O my chevalier!

   No wonder of it: shéer plód makes plough down sillion
Shine, and blue-bleak embers, ah my dear,
   Fall, gall themselves, and gash gold-vermillion.

   North Wales was the country of my soul because it
was the true Arcadia of wild nature. But when I
visited other areas of Wales and England and saw what
man was doing to other parts of our lovely country-
side with his mines and mills and factories and
refineries—with all their poisonous wastes—I was
appalled. Farmlands and meadows were disappearing
under slag heaps and the boot of man's treadmire toil.
Does God have more strength to renew than man has to
exploit? Are nature's resources more powerful and
plentiful than man's destructive energies?

The world is charged with the grandeur of God.
  It will flame out, like shining from shook foil;
  It gathers to a greatness, like the ooze of oil
Crushed. Why do men then now not reck his rod?
Generations have trod, have trod, have trod;
  And all is seared with trade; bleared, smeared with toil;
  And wears man's smudge and shares man's smell: the soil
Is bare now, nor can foot feel, being shod.

And for all this, nature is never spent;
  There lives the dearest freshness deep down things;
And though the last lights off the black West went
  Oh, morning, at the brown brink eastward, springs—
Because the Holy Ghost over the bent
  World broods with warm breast and with ah! bright wings.

My reverence for nature as a sacred trust flowed naturally and directly from my parents' Anglican faith, which had taught them—and through them, me—that we are here on earth as God's stewards to cherish and preserve as well as to use and develop His property. So it was no surprise to Mother to receive from her fledgling Jesuit a birthday letter with a small gift and a big thought:

> My dearest Mother,
> I send a duck's feather with my love. I practise at present the evangelical poverty which I soon hope to vow, but no one is ever so poor that he is not (without prejudice

to all the rest of the world) owner of the skies and stars and everything wild that is to be found on the earth, and out of this immense stock I make over to you my right to one particular. Give my best love to all.

Believe me, your loving son,
Gerard Hopkins.

One hundred and twenty years later, that duck's feather is still with that birthday letter.

&

"A wrong attitude toward nature implies, somewhere, a wrong attitude toward God." That wisdom comes from this solid member of the Establishment—a banker, editor, and critic as well as poet and playwright—memorialized here: Thomas Stearns Eliot, O.M. The "O.M." stands for Order of Merit, a British royal decoration, not a religious order. But Dylan Thomas liked to call him "Pope Eliot," because of his disapproval of Thomas' morals and poems.

A line from Eliot's "Four Quartets" is engraved on the tablet: "The communication of the dead is tongued with fire beyond the language of the living."

Neither the poetic nor the religious Eliot is tongued with fire. His poems, like his cats, are cool and detached. His God of choice is not the living God of Abraham and the prophets, of Job and of Jesus, but the rational deity of Job's friends, of Plato and Aristotle and Aquinas.

&

My earliest concept of God grew directly out of my childhood experience of my father's rearing of his lively brood of eight children. Manley Hopkins was a man of many interests and talents, a loving father who was never too busy with his work to give us children the love and the time we needed.

He enjoyed playing word games with us. There was no room in our home for harsh words. Only clever words, funny words, beautiful words, loving words. We basked in the warmth and affection of father's personality. Since he was the dominant male figure of my earliest years, whenever I prayed to our Heavenly Father, I imagined Him to be very like my earthly father.

I had to alter this image of God when I entered Highgate School at age ten and encountered the heavy-handed headmaster, John Bradley Dyne. He demanded absolute and fearful obedience, and to deny him that was to invite the lash of the rod. He was typical of a headmaster of his time: he believed that the only way to make English men out of English boys was to flog them often and with enthusiasm. I abhorred the practice.

One day Dyne stopped me on the school grounds and said: "You're not looking well, Hopkins. Your color is poor. Let me see your tongue. . . . Why, it's almost black! Are you ill?"

"Not really, sir. Another boy bet me I couldn't last a week without water. I have just won ten shillings, and that has made me feel better."

"What a stupid and dangerous prank. You could have seriously harmed your health. You must give back that money."

"I cannot give it back, sir. I won it fairly."

"You shall do as I say . . . or I shall flog you."

"You can flog me, sir, but I will not give it back."

He flogged me . . . and I kept the ten shillings.

After that, Dyne and I were repeatedly at odds, especially when I took on the cause of any boy whom he treated unjustly. Our vendetta came to a climax in a fierce exchange at the end of my last school year. In defending one of his victims, I was driven out of patience and cheeked Dyne wildly. He lost *his* head and blazed into me with his riding whip. During the final few weeks of the term, we avoided each other as much as possible.

Dyne left his mark on my theology as much as on my emotions and my body. God, I decided, was not only a loving father but also a scowling headmaster. Now I saw God as adversary-protector, as enemy-friend. Battling with God would be my prayer . . . contending, wrestling with God. For me he became the mysterious heavenly visitor who wrestled Jacob that strange night beside the river Jabbok.

Somehow I had to balance the two faces of the God I now knew. I could express this only in paradox: God was lightning and love, a winter and warm, a mighty master and a fond father.

I tried hard to be fair to God, but at times, under the stress of a black mood . . . when I felt my life and work to be nothing but a wasteland . . . I would cheek God as I had once cheeked headmaster Dyne:

> Thou art indeed just, Lord, if I contend
> With thee; but, sir, so what I plead is just.
> Why do sinners' ways prosper? and why must
> Disappointment all I endeavour end?

Wert thou my enemy, O thou my friend,
How wouldst thou worse, I wonder, than thou dost
Defeat, thwart me? Oh, the sots and thralls of lust
Do in spare hours more thrive than I that spend,

Sir, life upon thy cause. . . .

Over the years I learned that the quest for God is
endless. He is found . . . and lost . . . found again . . . and
lost again. He is a hidden God, and our faith is too
feeble to hold onto Him. The father with the sick child
in the Gospel spoke for all of us when he cried out to
Jesus for help: "I believe, Lord; help thou my unbelief."
That feeble faith would soon undergo its severest trial in
my life.

God is the *mysterium tremendum* . . . the final awesome
mystery . . . alone worthy of worship:

Be adored among men,
God, three-numberèd form;

. . . .

With an anvil-ding
And with fire in him forge thy will
Or rather, rather then, stealing as Spring
Through him, melt him but master him still:

. . . .

Make mercy in all of us, out of us all
Mastery, but be adored, but be adored King.

"Immortal diamond". . . it says here on my tablet. Two words from one of my last poems, "That Nature is a Heraclitean Fire and of the comfort of the Resurrection". . . . *That* has to be the most forbidding title ever given to a poem . . . sort of a baby dragon folded in the gate.

The last line of my tablet reads—"Buried at Glasnevin, Dublin." *Buried!* . . . *in Dublin!* . . . of all places! . . . *that* is a real bottom line for this John Bull of an Englishman. I, a passionate lover of all things English; how did I happen to end up in Dublin's public cemetery surrounded by the uncongenial monuments of Irish patriots . . . rebels, rather . . . like Wolfe Tone, Charles Parnell, Daniel O'Connell, Eamon De Valera?

Shortly before my fortieth birthday, Father Rector called me to his room and said that he had some good news for me. "You have been invited to become a fellow of the Royal University of Ireland and professor of Greek at University College, Dublin."

The news stunned me. "Ireland? Dublin?" I said. "You mean that place where all the Irish live? Well, it's a grand title, I admit, but without the grand thing."

He pointed out that it was an honor to be invited, that Ireland was not New Guinea, that the Irish Sea was not the Atlantic Ocean, that Dublin was only a short ferryboat ride from Liverpool, and that I would like the Irish Jesuits and the Irish people.

I agreed to think it over and let him know my decision. Reflection on my life up to this point cast me into a despondent mood. In the previous eight years I had had seven different assignments. My superiors had done their best to fit this square peg into one of their round holes. But I was simply ineffectual at whatever I was assigned to do.

As a parish priest in several different churches in various cities of England and Scotland, I was inept and awkward in my dealings with parishioners. My carefully worked out sermons put the people to sleep or made them snicker. Once I thought I had moved my congregation to tears, but closer inspection revealed that they were perspiring freely on that hot summer's day. Some were amused when I compared the Church to a cow, dispensing her life-giving sacraments the way a cow does her milk. Others were baffled when I rambled on at length, describing in glowing detail the beauty of the serpent and the fruit that tempted Eve in the Garden of Eden.

Despite my misgivings, I decided to accept the position in Dublin. In a letter to Bridges I disclosed my feelings about this decision: "I have long been Fortune's football and am blowing up the bladder of resolution big and buxom for another kick of her foot. I shall be sorry to leave England; but go or stay, there is no likelihood of ever doing anything to last."

Voltaire said that Jesuits meet without joy, part without sorrow, and die without regret. He may be right. We are always coming and going, arriving and departing, attached to no one, detached from all things. Permanence with us is cobweb, soapsud, and frost-feather permanence. If this Dublin assignment didn't work out, I could always ask for yet another change. And in such matters I had found my Jesuit superiors agreeable and helpful.

My superior proved to be right. I liked the Irish Jesuits. I liked the Irish people. But I disliked their politics. Their devotion to their Catholic religion — which is also mine, of course — has never interfered with their inherently rebellious natures.

I felt this keenly one Christmas morning as I was giving Holy Communion in a church outside Dublin. Many hundreds came forward to receive this sacrament with the unfailing devotion of the Irish, whose religion hangs suspended over their politics as the blue sky over the earth, both in one landscape but immeasurably remote and without contact or interference.

I made a special effort to understand the Irish problem and to be fair. It was true that Queen Victoria had neglected Ireland and that the Irish owed the royal family little gratitude. It was true that England had done much wrong to Ireland in the past, but now those wrongs for the most part had been righted . . . although the Irish would deny this. I really had no sympathy for the Irish nationalist movement, but I did support Home Rule for them, partly because it was just, partly because of the disorders that would result if it were denied, and partly because I considered the Irish an ungovernable people.

But no matter how pleasant my surroundings or how agreeable my companions, I could not rid myself of the feeling that I was in exile, a stranger and alone, separated from my dear England by the Irish Sea, separated from my family by religious differences, separated from Irish Catholics by political differences.

My creative work, crippled by some mysterious force of heaven or hell, had never won recognition or approval. It killed me to be time's eunuch, never to beget. It was a lonely life:

> To seem the stranger lies my lot, my life
> Among strangers. Father and mother dear,
> Brothers and sisters are in Christ not near
> And he my peace/my parting, sword and strife.

England, whose honour O all my heart woos, wife
To my creating thought, would neither hear
Me, were I pleading, plead nor do I. . . .

I am in Ireland now; now I am at a third
Remove. Not but in all removes I can
Kind love both give and get. Only what word

Wisest my heart breeds dark heaven's baffling ban
Bars or hell's spell thwarts. This to hoard unheard,
Heard unheeded, leaves me a lonely began.

I was readily given permission to take holidays in England and Wales to relieve the loneliness of my exile. Trouble was that I had to come back to Dublin where I was known as "the English Father" . . . not exactly a term of endearment in those unsettled days. During my third year in Ireland I began to feel a bit proud of myself because this was the first time in a decade that I had lasted more than one year in any assignment.

But in the fourth year this sack of foul clay began to come apart. Anxieties from the relentless pressure of work ground me down. First, a feeling of extreme fatigue and bodily weakness. Then, bouts of ill health that sent me to the infirmary. Finally, a persistent melancholy followed by a deepening depression.

What I had tolerated up to that time now became intolerable. The correction of exams, for one thing. Because of the terms of my appointment at the Royal University I had the task of correcting all examinations in Classics from all the colleges. This meant grading hundreds of exams during the academic year, a truly Herculean task.

There was nothing like 331 accounts of the Punic Wars—with trimmings—to sweat me down to my lees and low water mudflats with groans and yearnings. Since I had a very scrupulous bent, this became a form of refined torture for me. In my desire to be absolutely fair to each student, I would very carefully allot a fraction to each sentence in his exam and then end up in total confusion when I tried to add up all these fractions for the final grade.

In the meantime, members of the Examining Board were clamoring for results as I worked in my room with a wet towel wrapped around my aching head, trying to meet their deadlines. This was a recurring ordeal with no relief in sight.

My lectures became another source of constant anxiety. My students found them more and more tedious and boring. This made them inattentive and rude, talking and laughing amongst themselves. Some of the bolder ones became disruptive and ragged me.

When I was lecturing on the Trojan War, for example, and came to that part where Achilles killed Hector and viciously dragged his body around the walls of Troy, one of these students interrupted me to propose that I lie on the floor and let him drag me around the classroom by the heels to dramatize Hector's fate at Troy. The students loudly voiced their approval of this suggestion and turned the class into an uproar. I denied his request, of course; he had no real intellectual interest in Homer or his *Iliad.*

One day, my rector, Father Delaney, came into my room to discuss my problems and my health. He made one valuable suggestion. He urged me to write about my problems, my fears and my feelings, so that they would not fester in my mind uncommunicated. Words did relieve the pressure:

> My mind has thunderstorms
> That brood for heavy hours:
> Until they rain me words . . .

It worked—for a while. It was a temporary help, not a cure. As the weeks became months, I began to enter into a deeper course of desolation and terror. This made me fear madness. I felt at times that I was mad, even though my judgment was never affected. The fear of going mad is as frightening as madness itself:

> O the mind, mind has mountains; cliffs of fall
> Frightful, sheer, no-man-fathomed. Hold them cheap
> May who ne'er hung there. Nor does our small
> Durance deal with that steep or deep. Here! creep,
> Wretch, under a comfort serves in a whirlwind: all
> Life death does end and each day dies with sleep.

Guilt about the little I had done with my life gnawed at my conscience. I had always wanted to do a major literary work: an epic poem on the English Jesuit martyrs, featuring Edmund Campion. Nothing ever came of it. I did write an occasional short poem, but lacking the stimulus of publication, my output was slim. My correspondence lagged, chiefly for lack of energy on my part. All my go was gone. I was suffering the long defeat of having done nothing well:

Birds build—but not I build; no, but strain,
Time's eunuch, and not breed one work that wakes.
Mine, O thou lord of life, send my roots rain.

Nights meant nightmares. Horrible dreams would
startle me awake, agitated and sweating. Other times I
would be sleepless, filled only with a barren submission
to God's will and a loathing of my life:

I wake and feel the fell of dark, not day.
What hours, O what black hoŭrs we have spent
This night! what sights you, heart, saw; ways you went!
And more must, in yet longer light's delay.

With witness I speak this. But where I say
Hours I mean years, mean life. And my lament
Is cries countless, cries like dead letters sent
To dearest him that lives alas! away.

I am gall, I am heartburn. God's most deep decree
Bitter would have me taste: my taste was me;
Bones built in me, flesh filled, blood brimmed the curse. . . .

The lost are like this, and their scourge to be
As I am mine, their sweating selves; but worse.

In my agony I became that tall nun on the
Deutschland, searching the storm for any glimpse of
God's face. I could see nothing but the blinding snow
and the black-about air.

Comforter, where, where is your comforting?
Mary, mother of us, where is your relief?

Suddenly the storm clouds broke and showed a patch of the jay-blue heavens above . . . God's smile . . . lighting a lovely mile home. Then a wave of pity and patience would flood my heart and I would reproach myself for being so hard on myself, so impatient with God and resistant to His will:

> My own heart let me more have pity on; let
> Me live to my sad self hereafter kind,
> Charitable; not live this tormented mind
> With this tormented mind tormenting yet. . . .

&

> Patience, hard thing! the hard thing but to pray. . . .
> . . . .
> We hear our hearts grate on themselves: it kills
> To bruise them dearer. Yet the rebellious wills
> Of us we do bid God bend to him even so.

&

But the black mood would return . . . and I would be back again at the bottom of the dark pit wrestling with my adversary. Who was he? The two-faced God? My worser self? My father wearing the mask of headmaster Dyne? Jacob's mysterious wrestler? A creature of my feverish fancy . . . with lionlimbs and darksome, devouring eyes? Would I ever know?

And what was my life? Without aim, without spur, without help. And who was to blame for it? All my undertakings miscarried. I wished then for death. Yet if I had died then, I would have died imperfect, no master of myself. And that would have been the worst failure of all. "Dear God," I prayed, "look down on me. Let me not despair."

Not, I'll not, carrion comfort, Despair, not feast on thee;
Not untwist—slack they may be—these last strands of man
In me ór, most weary, cry *I can no more*. I can;
Can something, hope, wish day come, not choose not to be.

But ah, but O thou terrible, why wouldst thou rude on me
Thy wring-world right foot rock? lay a lionlimb against me? scan
With darksome devouring eyes my bruisèd bones? and fan,
O in turns of tempest, me heaped there; me frantic to avoid thee
     and flee?

Why? That my chaff might fly; my grain lie, sheer and clear.
Nay in all that toil, that coil, since (seems) I kissed the rod,
Hand rather, my heart lo! lapped strength, stole joy, would
     laugh, chéer.
Cheer whom though? The hero whose heaven-handling flung
     me, fóot tród
Me? or me that fought him? O which one? is it each one?
     That night, that year
Of now done darkness I wretch lay wrestling with (my God!)
     my God.

If the three years in Wales were the happiest of my life, then my last two years in Ireland were the unhappiest. At the age of forty-four I had been a Catholic for twenty-three years, a Jesuit for twenty-one, and a priest for twelve. I never regretted those decisions, never wavered in my allegiance, never looked back, once I had put my hand to the plough. But I was terribly frustrated as a working priest.

I lived and worked in Ireland for five years . . . five hard, wearying, wasting wasted years. In those years I did God's will . . . for the most part . . . and many, many examination papers. I did not blame the Irish for my problems. Outside of Ireland I would have been no better. Rather worse, probably.

I needed only one thing: a working health . . . a working strength. With that, any employment would have been tolerable or pleasant, enough for human nature. However, God did not see fit to endow me with bodily energy and cheerful spirits. I had to make do without them. But I did not despair, and I did keep my sanity. These were my victories.

᠎᠎᠎ː

June 8, 1889: The end came rather quickly and unexpectedly. One Dublin day in late spring, when there was growth in everything . . . and the bright wind boisterous had whipped the clouds into a dazzling whitewash against the glass-blue heavens . . . I came down with a high fever. A week passed before the doctor made a firm diagnosis.

I wrote to Mother: "My fever is a sort of typhoid. It is not severe, and my mind has never wandered for a moment. The nurse is first rate and every condition is present that could make a serious thing trifling. The only complaint I have is that food and medicine keep coming in like cricket balls. I have in fact every attention possible. Best love to all. I am your affectionate son, Gerard."

But I knew better. I was very ill. Shortly after that letter, my condition suddenly worsened. Father Rector notified my parents who rushed to my bedside. This upset me at first because I did not wish them to see me so helplessly stricken, but then I realized it was only fitting that they who had bent over me in my first sleep should watch over my last.

On Saturday morning, June 8th, shortly before noon, Father Rector began the traditional Catholic prayers for the dying. I could no longer speak, but I followed the words and responses of my mother and father, deeply grateful that they who had once opposed my acceptance of that faith were now, for these final moments, embracing that faith with me.

Death called at one o'clock. Thee, God, I come from, to Thee go. . . . My wrestling was over. God's terror no longer held me fast in life's wild wood. I was finally free . . . free of this coffin of weakness and dejection . . . free of this body of death.

Enough! the Resurrection,
A heart's-clarion! Away grief's gasping, joyless days, dejection.
Across my foundering deck shone
A beacon, an eternal beam. Flesh fade and mortal trash
Fall to the residuary worm; world's wildfire, leave but ash:
In a flash, at a trumpet crash,
I am all at once what Christ is, since he was what I am, and
This Jack, joke, poor potsherd, patch, matchwood, immortal
    diamond,
Is immortal diamond.

Epilogue

From the address by Peter Levi delivered on
December 8, 1975 in Westminster Abbey at the
ceremony memorializing Gerard Manley Hopkins in
Poets' Corner.

We are here today to commemorate the servant of God, Gerard Manley Hopkins, and to add his name to the company of the other English writers memorialized in the Poets' Corner of this great Abbey.

"Him that overcometh," says the Book of Revelation, "will I make a pillar in the temple of my God." Was Gerard Hopkins one of those who overcame, or was he one of the defeated? His was a restricted, unhappy life—let us not tell lies about him. He was eccentric and personal in his habits, he suffered intensely in ways we can hardly understand and he could hardly express, he belonged to a tiny and somewhat desperate minority in religion, he was not taken seriously as a poet or a scholar, he was tormented by scruples, he came close to despair. And when he died, he could feel the sap drying up in the branches of his life, he could hear the Spirit of God crying out in the long desert of the nineteenth century, he could hear the beating of iron wings.

He was terribly vulnerable, and yet strangely complete as a human being. Even in his most miserable hours, he possessed an unconfined freedom of spirit. This is what makes him so great a poet. It is not the curiosity of his studies, it is not the majestic decency of the lessons he learned from Ruskin, it is not even his astonishing technical skill or his moral authority. It is something like love. It is an inward community with the greenness of the earth, with the courageous boldness of an animal.

In the conversation of his soul he spoke freely, in his understanding of every natural thing he felt very freely. In his poems and writings we can sense this daring love, this God-given liberty.

Gerard Manley Hopkins is our father and brother in God. In him God has done his work and is still doing it. "Him that overcometh will I make a pillar in the temple of my God, and he shall go no more out: and I will write upon him the name of my God, and the name of the city of my God, which is new Jerusalem, which cometh down out of heaven from my God; and I will write upon him my new name."

Appendix

On First Looking into Hopkins' Poems

Even if a definitive or a satisfactory biography of Hopkins were available today, the best approach to Hopkins would still be through his poems in the company of an authoritative guide. Fortunately, that guide is available. He is Norman H. MacKenzie, the present official editor of Hopkins' poems.

Anything this sensible Canadian scholar writes about Hopkins and his poems is totally reliable and worthy of close attention. He is not beguiled by theories. All his interpretations are based on a healthy and profound understanding of the text of the poems and their evolution in Hopkins' life and mind. He brings to his task a combination of gifts rarely found together in a single scholar: humility, accuracy, insight, common sense, and readability.

Two books are essential for this approach to Hopkins with MacKenzie as the guide. The first is *The Poems of Gerard Manley Hopkins*, Fourth Edition, edited by W. H. Gardner and N. H. MacKenzie, Oxford University Press, 2d printing, 1973, paper, $9.95. This fourth edition brings together all of Hopkins' known poems in their chronological development. The second book, its numbering synchronized with the numbers in the first book, is *A Reader's Guide to Gerard Manley Hopkins* by Norman H. MacKenzie, Cornell University Press, Ithaca, N.Y., 1981, paper, $13.95. This book is a treasure, an indispensable *vade mecum* for the study of the most challenging of poets.

Two other books deserve notice. One is *Gerard Manley Hopkins: Selected Prose*, edited by Gerald Roberts, Oxford University Press, 1980, paper, $10.95. This excellent selection from Hopkins' voluminous correspondence and writings reveals Hopkins in his human dimensions. The other is *Gerard Manley Hopkins: Poems and Prose*, edited by W. H. Gardner, Penguin Books, 1953, $5.95. This is recommended for those who need to save money for less important things than poetry.

One final note: Hopkins advised that his poems were written to be spoken by the tongue and heard by the ear as well as read by the eyes. Heed his advice.